A PICTORIAL HISTORY OF
SANTA CLAUS

By the same author

The English Sunrise

A PICTORIAL HISTORY OF

SANTA CLAUS

*

BRIAN RICE

CHATTO & WINDUS

LONDON

First published in 1995

1 3 5 7 9 10 8 6 4 2

Copyright © Brian Rice 1995

Brian Rice has asserted his right under the Copyright, Designs
and Patents Act, 1988 to be identified as the author of this work.

First published in Great Britain in 1995 by
Chatto & Windus Limited
Random House, 20 Vauxhall Bridge Road,
London SW1V 2SA

Random House Australia (Pty) Limited
20 Alfred Street, Milson's Point, Sydney
New South Wales 2061, Australia

Random House New Zealand Limited
18 Poland Road, Glenfield
Auckland 10 New Zealand

Random House South Africa (Pty) Limited
P O Box 337, Bergvlei, South Africa

Random House UK Limited Reg. No. 954009

Papers used by Random House UK Limited are natural, recyclable
products made from wood grown in sustainable forests. The
manufacturing processes conform to the environmental regulations
of the country of origin

A CIP catalogue record for this book is available from
the British Library

ISBN 0 7011 6526 X

To Sarah
who makes most things possible

INTRODUCTION

This book represents the first serious attempt to document the portrayal of Santa Claus, St Christopher, or Father Christmas as he is variously known, in the history of Western Art. If the first painting in this book is genuine, we can assume that he began life as an Egyptian Household God, before 1000 BC. By the 13th Century, paintings of Santa begin to appear regularly, and from that time to the present, the figure of Santa Claus with a bushy white beard, red cloak and hat trimmed with white fur becomes a regular subject for artists.

In the Medieval period he is often depicted as a saint, with halo, or as an angel. In the 15th Century, some artists seem to question his sexuality, but by the sixteenth Century he is restored to his traditional role, delivering presents on Christmas on Christmas Eve. A plot by the Catholic Church to convince the populace that Santa was dead evidently failed, as artists continued to depict a cheerful, healthy Santa. Spanish artists in the 17th and 18th Century had certain problems with the benign image of Santa; in the early 19th Century, while English artists depicted the spiritual and mystic nature of Santa, French painters began to characterise him as a lecher and drinker, or buffoon, appearing unsuitably dressed for mid-summer. This defamatory trend continued into the 20th Century, when he is pictured sneaking out of brothels and leering drunkenly in the theatres and bars of Paris. A number of artists painted Santa as a woman or in women's clothes, but critics have pointed out that this probably reflects on the artists themselves and was not necessarily related to Santa's own behaviour or habits. There is no evidence that he was a cross-dresser and breast implants were simply not available until the late 20th century.

For the purposes of this book, we conclude our survey at approximately 1930. This is not because contemporary artists have ceased to be interested in painting Santa, but rather that there is too much 20th Century Santa art to be effectively assessed and documented. The dividing line between sincere and affectionate portrayal and sentimental commercialism is a slender one. Moreover, it has always been difficult to make an objective judgement on the art of one's own time. Quite possibly, at this moment, an aspiring young artist is formulating plans to exhibit Santa, suitably prepared, in a glass tank of formaldehyde. The next time you see someone in red robes and bushy white beard, will it be an impecunious actor earning a crust, or a Performance Artist paying tribute to the greatest performance artist of all time, Santa Claus?

In concluding, we should ask ourselves the question: was Santa himself an artist? Some believe he was – he certainly appears to have been a close acquaintance of many of history's great painters. Possibly he was a talented Sunday painter who liked to mingle with the great artists of the past. As none of his paintings has ever been seen, we have no idea of their merit. Surely the job of being Santa Claus must have kept him busy most of the year, apart from the occasional visit to the pub or the Salon of the Rue des......but that's for another day.

In this painting from the floor of the coffin of the Theban official Ahmose, dated circa 1050 B.C., we see the first known depiction of Santa Claus. Experts disagree about its authenticity. Some, pointing to the slight difference in style, believe that the head is a later addition.

10

By the 13th Century depictions of Santa were beginning to appear more frequently, as in this painting by Giotto di Bondone (1266–1377).

12

In this illuminated manuscript, part of the *De Lisle Psalter,* Santa Claus is portrayed attending the Coronation of the Virgin.

14

A detail from an address in Latin verse circa 1335–1340, showing Santa playing the violin, flanked by two rather bored looking angels. (Artist unknown).

16

Few experts have noticed the figure of Santa Claus amongst the many angels in the famous 'Wilton Diptych'. This is surprising, as his bright red robe stands out clearly in this predominantly blue painting (circa 1395).

In this well known painting, 'The Arnolfini Wedding', by Jan van Eyck, Santa is in the background, but his sack of toys takes prominence of place. Possibly Santa was thought to deliver wedding presents in the 15th Century.

A charming 15th Century painting by Hans Memling (active 1465-1494) of Santa amongst a group of 'Angel Musicians'. Note that Santa was also portrayed with angel wings in this period.

22

A bizarre scene from a 15th Century French Book of Hours, where peasants appear to be stoning Santa. Did he forget their presents?

Et facere sentia
nuccth vpi mar
hr kato stepst
ho quī m̄ nūcō sānctorū̄

In 'Portrait of a Girl' by Ghirlandaio (1449-1494), painted in 1480, the subject wears a locket bearing the face of Santa, which shows how popular he had become by this time.

'The Birth of Santa' by Sandro Botticelli (1447–1510). One of his greatest paintings.

A touching portrait painted in 1538, by Albrecht Dürer (1471-1528) of a rather old and frail, but nevertheless smiling Santa.

A rather effeminate portrait of Santa Claus painted around 1550–1515, by Raphael (1483–1520).

A painting by the 16th Century artist Pieter Brueghel the Elder (1530–1569), showing an apparently unconcerned Santa Claus delivering presents, while the 'Massacre of the Innocents' takes place behind him.

In this portrait of George Gisze, painted in 1532 by Hans Holbein the Younger (1497–1543), Santa Claus is pictured creeping up behind him to surprise him with presents while he opens his Christmas cards.

36

Santa Claus appears behind a woman as she addresses Christmas cards at her table. Painted by Jan Vermeer of Delft (1632-1675).

It would be strange if Rembrandt (1606-1669) had ignored such a good subject as Santa. In this painting of 1655 he is shown riding through the night to deliver presents. (No reindeer and sledge in the 17th century.)

40

Johannes Vermeer (1665–1670) painted this allegorical work of an artist, possibly himself, painting the portrait of Santa Claus.

42

This great painting by Velasquez (1599–1660) which hangs in the Prado, depicts Santa handing out presents to a group of soldiers at 'The Surrendering of Breda'.

In another famous painting by Velasquez, Venus sees Santa Claus in the Mirror. Also known as 'The Rokeby Santa'.

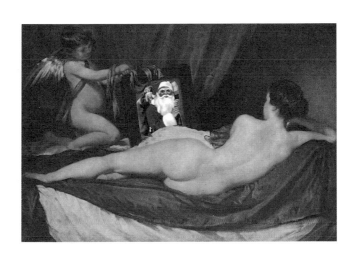

This curious painting by El Greco (1541–1614), 'The Burial of Santa Claus', is thought to have been a commission for the Church, painted in an attempt to convince a gullible Spanish populace that Santa was dead.

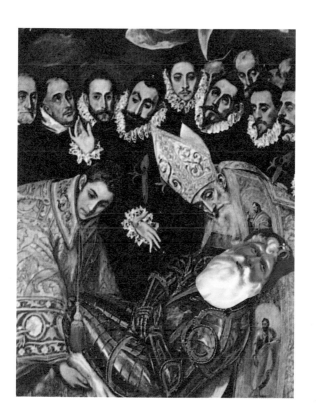

The Dutch artist Pieter de Hoogh (1629–1684) painted this scene of Santa arriving at the door of a rather grand house and handing over presents to the lady.

50

The woman of this house, along with her daughter, is about to be surprised by Santa Claus dropping from the chimney. Another painting by Pieter de Hoogh.

Frans Hals (1580–1666) painted this famous portrait, 'The Laughing Santa', circa 1623.

The French artist Jean Siméon Chardin (1699–1779) made this painting in 1735 of a young girl checking her presents from a list while Santa waits impatiently.

Francisco Goya (1746–1828) depicted an apparently deranged Santa Claus wielding a bread knife. One of several macabre images of Santa by this artist.

Another of Goya's famous 'black paintings' in which a rather jolly Santa overlooks two old people eating their Christmas lunch of soup.

In this painting by Goya, Santa Claus is being held up by a group of soldiers and forced to hand over a box of presents, while the intended recipients cry in despair.

G oya's painting of Santa Claus in drag, although some observers believe it to be a painting of a woman in a false Santa beard and hat.

Depictions of Santa outside of Europe are rare. This wood-block print of Santa Claus in traditional costume, by the 18th Century Japanese artist Torii Kiyomitsu II, is almost unique.

S ir Henry Raeburn R.A. (1756–1823), the leading Scots painter of his day, was responsible for this rather gnome-like portrait of Santa in a typical Scottish landscape.

This splendid painting of Santa Claus on a Dapple Grey Horse, complete with his sack of toys, was painted between 1760-65 by George Stubbs (1724-1806).

In 1794–5 Sir Henry Raeburn painted a second portrait of Santa, this time in full Highland costume.

This William Blake (1757–1827) painting, circa 1795, in which Santa Claus encounters an Evil Angel while delivering presents to a young child, was his only portrayal of Santa.

A beautiful rural scene by the mystic Samuel Palmer (1805–1881). Santa leads a procession of villagers home from church on Christmas Eve.

76

In this detail from 'The Death of Sardanapalus' painted in 1827 by Ferdinand Victor Eugène Delacroix (1798-1863), a semi-naked Santa Claus appears to have been caught in a highly compromising situation. Typically French.

After much painstaking research, the Pre-Raphaelite painter, Dante Gabriel Rossetti (1828-1882), became convinced that the authentic colours for Santa's robe and hat were blue. Most other artists ignored him.

80

Edouard Manet (1832–1883), made
this painting of Santa playing the fife
in 1866.

82

Manet made this painting in 1868-69, in which Santa, depicted as St. Nicholas with Mitre and Bishop's Crook, appears on a balcony with two rather bored ladies.

84

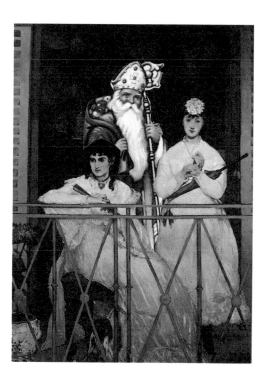

A summer scene: 'Santa in the Blue Boat' by Claude Monet (1840-1926). Santa Claus looks rather ridiculous in his fur trimmed coat, clutching presents in mid-July.

86

Despite the idyllic weather, this is a painting of Christmas Day bathers being watched by Santa. Painted 1883–84 by Georges Seurat (1859–1891).

Some experts think that this painting by Paul Cezanne (1839–1906) may be a self-portrait.

In this Renoir of 1870–80, look carefully in the crowd and, despite 'The Umbrellas', you will spot Santa, out shopping and attempting to be incognito.

Hilaire Germain Edgar Degas (1834–1917) painted this jolly laughing portrait of Santa in a shawl, relaxing in his favourite armchair on Boxing Day.

94

In this painting of 1890, Cezanne makes Santa Claus look like the bearded lady.

This painting by Henri de Toulouse-Lautrec (1846-1901), 'Santa Claus in the Salon of the Rue des Moulins 1894', depicts a rather furtive Santa. Has he been delivering presents or receiving favours?

A charming painting by Berthe Morisot (1841–1895), in which Santa leaves presents beside a baby's cradle.

100

Another painting by Manet called 'Santa Buys a Round', depicting the off-duty Santa as a fun-loving chap who likes a laugh and a beer…or two.

Aportrait by Paul Cezanne: sympathetic, but portraying Santa as rather old and frail.

A painting by Claude Monet (1840–1926): 'Santa at Vetheuil: Sunshine and Snow'.

Another landscape painting showing Santa Claus waiting for the citizens of Arles to go to bed, in order that he may get on with delivering their presents. Painted by Vincent Van Gogh (1853-1890).

This painting is also by Van Gogh. It is usually interpreted as a portrait of Vincent himself, as Santa.

Paul Gauguin (1848-1903) probably missed the French Christmas Festivities in far away Tahiti, and painted this dusky Santa Claus as a therapeutic reminder.

112

Did Gauguin take drugs in his Tahitan Paradise? In this painting he seems to confuse the native women with a vision of Santa.

Georges Rouault (1871–1958), portrays Santa Claus in almost religious splendour in this painting entitled 'Head of Santa'.

This wonderful decorative painting of Santa Claus being thanked by a grateful recipient of gifts is by Gustav Klimt (1862–1918).

Amadeo Modigliani (1184–1920) painted this portrait of Santa Claus in his gardening clothes, in 1917, and rather unkindly called it 'Santa, the Little Peasant'.

120